Merry
[signature]

LOVE/LIFE

BILL HOWARD

Charleston, AR
COBB PUBLISHING
2023

Published in the United States of America by:

Cobb Publishing
704 East Main St.
Charleston, AR 72993
Editor@Cobb Publishing.com
www.CobbPublishing.com
479.747.8372
Interior and Cover design by Bradley S. Cobb

All Scripture from KJV unless otherwise noted

ISBN: 978-1-960858-99-3

DEDICATION

To my loving wife, Juanita, and to her alone who is the source of encouragement and the reason for the writing of this book.

CHAPTER 1

Several years ago, there was a popular song entitled "Love is a Many Splendored Thing," another was "Love Makes the World Go Round." That is a statement that is literally the truth. If it wasn't for love, there would not be a world. The word "love" is an habitually mis-used word. It has in many instances become a crutch word or a helper word when others would more likely express what we intend, but we have accustomed ourselves to use "love" to cover a significant number of feelings or emotions. For example, I might say, "I love Brussels Sprouts," when what I intended to express is, "I can tolerate them occasionally." "I love that movie," but what I intended was "I liked it and enjoyed it." Because the true meaning of love is so weighty and strong, there are times when other words are more fitting: adore, like, enjoy, admire, fancy, dote, relish, just to consider a few. There are many dozens more, but these make the point. There are times when love is simply not the best choice of word in making a statement or to express a feeling. So, we would like to consider a few thoughts about the word love and the truly heart-felt meaning of the expression of love.

Let us not misunderstand; there is no intention to disparage the word love. It is a beautiful word, and it is a very strong and meaningful word. The importance, the efficacy of love stems from its creator, the loving God

1

in Heaven. The meaning of love, and words closely akin to it, is used hundreds of times in the **B**ible. In the Greek language, the highest and most meaningful word for love is the word *Agape* which corresponds to the Hebrew *Ahaba* or *Aheb*. These words express the kind of love God has for mankind and that one would feel for children or spouse.

We can gain understanding of the word *Ahaba* and how meaningful it is from Deuteronomy 6:5. Moses told Israel, "Thou shalt love the Lord thy God with all thine heart, with all thine soul, and with all thy might." Jesus repeated this passage when the Pharisee lawyer asked Him which was the greatest commandment in the law (Matthew 22:37). The whole person, body, soul, and spirit is to love God. Anything less is unacceptable and carries with it a threat of ruin.

God is the source of everything that exists because He is the creator. Everything we can hope to be, all that we are, all that we have and everything for which we have hope are in the living God. Comprehending this, we can love God above everything else and with the greatest intent possible. We love Him because He first loved us (1 John 4:19). Had it not been for the love which God has for His creation, there would have been many more destroyed for failing to do as the Lord has decreed. He is a loving God, but He is no respecter of persons (Acts 10:34). We are all equal in His eyes. If we do not heed His word, there will be consequences. When we comprehend the overwhelming love that our

Father has for us, we can understand the real meaning of love and know how we are to love God in return for His loving and blessing us.

This love God has for His creation is a spontaneous love. Not something which was due to mankind, not something drawn out of the Father because of anything that mankind was or wasn't, nor something deserved. It was and is love freely given.

> *"The Lord did not set His love upon you, nor choose you, because you were more in number than any people; for you were the fewest of all people: but because the Lord loved you, and because he would keep the oath which He had sworn unto your fathers, hath the Lord brought you out with a mighty hand, and redeemed you out of the house of bondmen, from the hand of Pharaoh king of Egypt" (Deuteronomy 7:7-8).*

Some forty years or so before this statement, Moses relayed a message from God to the Israelites:

> *"Remember this day, in which ye came out from Egypt, out of the house of bondage; for by strength of hand the Lord brought you out from this place: there shall no leavened bread be eaten" (Exodus 13:3).*

God took them from bondage because He loved them and did not wish for them to suffer further.

> *"And the Lord thy God will bring thee into the land which thy fathers possessed, and thou shall*

3

possess it; and He will do thee good, and multi-
ply thee above thy fathers. And the Lord thy God
will circumcise thine heart, and the heart of thy
seed, to love the Lord thy God with all thine
heart, and will all thy soul, that thou mayest
live" (Deuteronomy 30:5-6).

This is God loving mankind.

From perhaps some of the oldest biblical writings, the question comes from a man in the throes of suffering: Job expressed a thought which he had been pondering. "What is man, that thou shouldest magnify him? And that thou shouldest set thine heart upon him?" (Job 7:17). We are not going to explore Job's situation but just give some thought to his question. The Psalmist puzzled over the same question: "What is man, that thou are mindful of him?" and "Lord, what is man that thou are mindful of him?" (Psalm 8:4, 144:3). It is not a far-fetched idea that Job and the Psalmist would wonder about God and His wondrous love of mankind. After all, God is Sovereign, the Lord of Lords, High Priest, the mighty King, the Holy Father. There is no position known that is higher than God. He is the omnipotent God that created the Universe, the galaxies therein, the world and man. Nothing exists which was not created by God. So, they might tend to be curious; why is such a magnificent being concerned with man? The answer is simple; He loves the creature of His creation. Even though the Israelites were time and time again turning away from God, He still loved them. At one point, He allowed Jerusalem to be destroyed and the Jews scattered because of their disobedience, but God made a way of Israel being restored. Why? Because of the prodigious love He had for the people. Jeremiah, alluding to that restoration, quoted God: "The Lord hath appeared of old unto me, saying, Yea, I have loved thee with an everlasting love: therefore, with lovingkindness have I drawn thee. Again, I will build thee" (Jeremiah 31:3-4a). It is difficult for man to fathom God's ways at times, but He said: "For my thoughts are not your thoughts, neither are your ways my ways, saith the Lord. For as the heavens are higher than the earth, so are my ways higher than your ways, and my thoughts than your thoughts" (Isaiah 55:8-9). We will now see the actual profundity of God's love for mankind.

John indicates the depth of God's love: "Herein is love, not that we loved God, but that He loved us, and sent his Son to be the propitiation for our sins" (1 John 4:10). Propitiation is an offering, a sacrifice for payment, atonement for the purpose of reconciliation. Sin destroys the relationship between man and God; for man to be reconciled to God, there had to be a sacrifice. The writer of the Hebrew letter wrote: "I (Jesus) come to do thy will O God," and, "By the which will we are sanctified through the offering of the body of Jesus Christ, once for all" (Hebrews 10:9a-10). Sanctified means freed from sin, made Holy, and through this comes reconciliation.

With our finite human mind is it even possible for us to comprehend the extent of God's love? He gave his son; think about this as we look at one of our children or a loved one. John tells us in one of the most memorized and quoted scriptures:

"For God so loved the world that He gave His only begotten Son, that whosoever believeth in Him should not perish, but have everlasting life. For God sent not His Son into the world to condemn the world; but that the world through Him might be saved" (John 3:16-17).

The Apostle Paul wrote to Titus:

"the kindness and love of God our Savior toward man appeared, not by works of righteousness which we have done, but according to His mercy He saved us, by the washing of regeneration, and renewing of the Holy Spirit: which He shed on us abundantly through Jesus Christ our Savior" (Titus 3:4-6).

Jesus said of himself: "Just as the son of man did not come to be served, but to serve, and to give His life a ransom for many" (Matthew 20:28). Paul wrote: "There is therefore no condemnation to them which are in Christ Jesus, who walk not after the flesh, but after the Spirit" (Romans 8:1). When we are separated from God, we are living a life that is sinful, we are concerned with the things of the world, living a life contrary to what God expects from us. However, when we accept God's terms of salvation, we no longer walk in the ways of the world but are in Christ Jesus, led by the Spirit, and are reconciled with God. Paul told the Galatians: "This I say then, walk in the Spirit, and ye shall not fulfill the lust of the flesh" (Galatians 5:16). More than a thousand years before God sent His Son, David already understood what it meant to know God's love.

> *"Give thanks to the Lord, call on His name; make known among the nation what He has done; sing to Him, sing praise to Him; tell of all His wonderful acts. Glory in His name; let the hearts of those who seek the Lord rejoice; then, Give thanks to the Lord, for He is good; His love endures forever" (1 Chronicles 16:8-10 and 16:34, NIV).*

We will have more to consider on this subject a bit later in the writing.

CHAPTER 2

We have given thought to the love of God for all of mankind and His concern that His creation was living in sin, because of which man had created a chasm between himself and God. Man had to be reconciled with God or be lost. It was incumbent on God, if it was going to happen, to set in motion the means for that reconciliation in order that man could be saved from sin. He devised this way because of love. "And we have known and believed the love that God hath to us. God is love; and he that dwelleth in love dwelleth in God, and God in him" (1 John 4:16).

God accomplished this way of salvation by giving His Son Jesus unto the world to be a sacrifice. Let's give some consideration to His giving His Son and why. Could there not be a different way, a better way that would save Jesus from the suffering the humiliation and the brutal death by crucifixion? At the time of Jesus' baptism by John, God said, "This is my beloved Son, in whom I am well pleased" (Matthew 3:17). John stated: "The Father loveth the Son, and hath given all things into His hand" (John 3:35). Paul referred to Jesus as God's dear Son (Colossians 1:13). When Christ was transfigured on the mountain, again God said: "This is my beloved Son: in whom I am well pleased; hear ye Him" (Matthew 17:5). Jesus said of the Father: "thou lovedst me before the foundation of the world" (John 17:24).

What source of love could be greater than the love of God for His only Son? Still, God offered His Son to be a sacrifice: do we have a riddle or puzzle here? In no way, everything since the beginning of time has been orchestrated by God; there can be no question, no puzzle about what takes place. Neither can there be a question of God's love for Jesus. If there must be a sacrifice, and there had to be, then the sacrifice made had to be without spot or blemish, it must be perfect, and Jesus was the only perfect being without spot or blemish, so God made Jesus to be the sacrifice. The Hebrew writer said that the blood of bulls and goats could not take away sin (Hebrews 10:4). Then if animal sacrifice was not acceptable it had to be human—and that left only Christ as the one eligible. Again, the Hebrew writer: "but now once in the end of the world hath he (Jesus) appeared to put away sin by the sacrifice of himself" (Hebrews 10:26b). Also, "By the which will, we are sanctified through the offering of the body of Jesus Christ" (Hebrews 10:10). So, the one without blemish is to become blemished with the sins of the world in order that sins can be forgiven. Peter said that Christ did suffer and die for all guilty sinners, yet He Himself was without sin.

"For Christ also hath once suffered for sins, the just for the unjust, that He might bring us to

God, being put to death in the flesh, but quick-
ened by the Spirit" (1 Peter 3:18).

"For this purpose the Son of God was mani-
fested, that He might destroy the works of the
Devil" (1 John 3:8).

Paul wrote:

"For He [God] hath made him [Christ] to be
sin for us who knew no sin; that we might be
made the righteousness of God in Him" (2 Corinthians 5:21).

Again the words of Paul:

"Christ hath redeemed us from the curse of the
law, being made a curse for us: for it is written,
cursed is every one that hangeth on a tree" (Galatians 3:13).

Peter wrote to Christians:

"For even hereunto were ye called; because
Christ also suffered for us, leaving us an example, that ye should follow His steps: Who did no
sin, neither was guile found in His mouth: Who,
when He was reviled, reviled not again; when
He suffered, He threatened not; but committed
himself to Him that judgeth righteously: Who
His own self bare our sins in His own body on
the tree, that we, being dead to sins, should live
unto righteousness: by whose stripes ye were
healed" (1 Peter 2:21-24).

These thoughts are the fulfillment of the prophecy Isaiah made more than seven hundred years before Christ was known on earth.

"Surely He hath borne our griefs, and carried our sorrows; yet we did esteem Him stricken, smitten of God, and afflicted. But He was wounded for our transgressions, He was bruised for our iniquities: the chastisement of our peace was upon Him; and with His stripes we are healed" (Isaiah 53:4-5).

So, there it is, the sacrifice of one who was without sin to bring salvation for the sinners of all times. Jesus did this happily, He was aware of what was coming, the beatings, the suffering, the cruel and brutal death on the cross, yet He did it with joy. The writer of the Hebrew letter wrote that we are: "looking unto Jesus the author and finisher of our faith; who for the joy that was set before Him endured the cross, despising the shame, and is set down at the right hand of the throne of God" (Hebrews 12:2). What could we imagine that, from the suffering He endured, would bring joy? There are three things that come to mind immediately in answer to that question.

1. *He was doing the will of His Father*. He said that God's will would come before His. He stated: "I can of mine own self do nothing: as I hear I judge: and my judgment is just; because I seek not mine own will, but the will of the Father which hath sent me" (John 5:30). Another time He said: "Therefore doth my Father love

11

me, because I lay down my life, that I might take it again" (John 10:17). Jesus was obedient to the Father and was happy; in doing that, it would bring Him joy.

2. *He came to "save His people from their sins"* (Matthew 1:21). The world was lost because of sin and by the death of one man untold millions of people will have the opportunity to avail themselves of the saving blood of Jesus Christ. Man can be in the kingdom of God on earth and have certainty of being in Heaven with God forever. This certainly would make Jesus happy knowing this could be possible because of His suffering.

3. *Jesus would be joyous when all was accomplished, and He would return to heaven in the presence of God.* His final words before His death were "It is finished." He had fulfilled the will of His Father, His life was not finished, He would be resurrected according to God's plan and return to His honored place at the right hand of God. Jesus said:

> *"As the father hath loved me, so have I loved you, continue ye in my love. If ye keep my commandments, ye shall abide in my love; even as I have kept my Father's commandments, and abide in His love.... Greater love hath no man than this, that a man lay down his life for his friends" (John 15:9-10 and 13).*

God loved His Son, He also loved mankind. His mercy rescued both.

12

CHAPTER 3

These are the words of Moses to the Israelites about fourteen hundred fifty years before the advent of Christ on earth. The Israelites had wandered the wilderness for forty years and were at the point of entering the promised land. "And thou shalt love the Lord thy God with all thine heart, and with all thy soul, and with all thy might" (Deuteronomy 6:5). The Israelites had every reason to show infinite love for the one true God who had cared for them for so long and was about to give to them the promise made to Abraham many years ago. A little earlier Moses had reminded them what the Lord had said. "I am the Lord thy God, which brought thee out of the land of Egypt, from the house of bondage" (Deuteronomy 5:6). Despite the many times the people had ill-treated God and His wishes, turned their back on Him, disobeyed Him, He still loved them and cared for them, and Moses was reminding them that they should love God with all their being.

> *"And now Israel, what doth the Lord thy God require of thee, but to fear the Lord thy God, to walk in all His ways, and to love Him, and to serve the Lord thy God with all thy heart and with all thy soul" (Deuteronomy 10:12).*

This was always their duty but not always fulfilled.

A very few years after this, Joshua was speaking with the Reubenites, the Gadites, and part of the tribe of Manasseh, commending them for their faithfulness.

"Ye have kept all that Moses the servant of the Lord commanded you, and have obeyed my voice in all that I commanded you: Ye have not left your brethren these many days unto this day, but have kept the charge of the commandment of the Lord your God. And now the Lord your God hath given rest unto your brethren, as He promised them: therefore now return ye, and get you unto your tents, and unto the land of your possession, which Moses the servant of the Lord gave you on the other side Jordan. But take diligent heed to do the commandment and the law, which Moses the servant of the Lord charged you, to love the Lord your God, and to walk in all His ways, and to keep His commandments, and to cleave unto Him, and to serve Him with all your heart and with all your soul" (Joshua 22:2-5).

Prior to Joshua's death, he exhorted them again: "Take good heed therefore unto yourselves, that ye love the Lord your God" (Joshua 23:11).

Then, as today, we are bound to love our God, to respect His will and do His bidding. If one truly loves and respects God and intends to be obedient to His wishes, it will be evident in the lives which others see in us. Jesus reminded all of us of this truth as He spoke from the mountain.

> *"You are the salt of the earth. But what good is salt if it has lost its flavor? Can you make it salty again? It will be thrown out and trampled underfoot as worthless. You are the light of the world, like a city on a hilltop that cannot be hidden. No one lights a lamp and then puts it under a basket. Instead, a lamp is placed on a stand, where it gives light to everyone in the house. In the same way, let your good deeds shine out for all to see, so that everyone will praise your heavenly Father"* (Matthew 5:13-16, NLT).

The purpose of light is to overpower darkness. Our doing God's bidding, our good works, our good deeds, it is that power that shines for people to know of God. We as His children do not do these things for our own aggrandizement, but that others can see the works of a Christian and glorify our Father in heaven.

Along with admonishing the people of their need to love God, Moses also reminded them of their sins while he was on the mountain to receive the commandments of God. Having Aaron make a calf of gold and claim that it was the God that led them out of bondage was typical of their disobedience. If we love God, we will not deliberately sin; we will honor Him, praise Him, glorify Him and give to Him our unfailing love. The Israelites failed in this too many times, and we today are

15

at times guilty of the same. We tend to idolize the wrong things and become lax in our attention to God. This is unacceptable; we must constantly remind ourselves that this is God, this is *our* God, the *true and living* God. It is unthinkable and totally wrong to allow a higher affection to be placed in any other people, place or thing. We must reserve and exhibit our greatest love for God.

The people were warned that some would come along to draw them away from God saying:

> *"Let us go after other gods, which thou hast not known, and let us serve them; thou shalt not hearken unto the words of that prophet, or that dreamer of dreams: for the Lord your God proveth you, to know whether ye love the Lord your God with all your heart and with all your soul" (Deuteronomy 13:2b-3).*

So, what does this mean to those people many centuries ago? *Do not be led away from God. There are those who will tempt you but do not be misled. God knows you and will test you to determine your love for him.*

From that time until this day nothing has changed in His will. We are to love God with all our heart and all our soul. Jesus repeated these very words when the Pharisee lawyer tried to tempt Him with a question.

> *"'Master, which is the greatest commandment in the law'? Jesus said unto him, 'Thou shalt love the Lord thy God with all thy heart, and*

with all thy soul and with all my mind'" (Mat-
thew 22:36-37).

Only loving God to this extent shows that we truly do love Him; when we truly love Him, we will always be God's friend and be richly blessed in so doing. While man will never be capable of loving as God loves, as a believer we will be a partaker of all the wonderful blessings He has for those who seek Him.

From the time of Adam and Eve, Satan has been ever present, stalking God's people, his greatest delight is seeing a child of God fall away and cease loving and obeying God. Peter warned Christians of this danger. "Be sober, be vigilant; because your adversary the devil, as a roaring lion, walketh about, seeking whom he may devour" (1 Peter 5:8). Two thousand years later the same threat is ever present. Whatever temptations people had thousands of years ago, we have far more in the present day. The opportunities to adopt idols which we worship, idols that take us away from our love for God, have been multiplied many times over. We witness the truth of this when we look at the fallen world in which we live. Morality has tanked, lies are substituted for truth any time a lie will accomplish the desired result, there is more hatred exhibited in our world today than ever before, evil is rampant, broken homes because of alcohol and drugs, one parent families because of divorce, rioting and destruction of property, and it increases exponentially with each passing day in our present world. The job we have, our stocks and bonds, where we buy our clothes, the car we drive and the house we live in are just a few of the idols we pursue today, and for each hour we allot to these pursuits is an hour taken from our dedication to pleasing and loving our God. We seek after those things which are temporary and in the end will have no value whatsoever. We can become slaves to these valueless tokens of success. We can strive for them, but when we have gained them there is no gratification.

As long as we are seeking contentment with things, we will be disappointed. They cannot bring us peace, joy, happiness or satisfaction. What comes of this is only stress, anxiety and endless worry. Jesus said when He was speaking on the mount:

> *"And why take ye thought for raiment? Consider the lilies of the field, how they grow; they toil not, neither do they spin: and yet I say unto you, that even Solomon in all his glory was not arrayed like one of these" (Matthew 6:28-29).*

If this is true, and we know it is because Jesus said it, why do we strive for those things which have no lasting value? We saddle ourselves with the burden of gaining when all we need to do is love God and trust Him for our needs. James, the brother of Jesus wrote of this subject:

> *"Look here, you who say, 'Today or tomorrow we are going to a certain town and will stay there a year. We will do business there and make*

18

*a profit.' How do you know what your life will
be like tomorrow? Your life is like the morning
fog, it's here a little while, then it's gone. What
you ought to say is, if the Lord wants us to, we
will live and do this or that" (James 4:13-15,
NLT).*

In life, we have no guarantees, we have no assurance
of anything beyond the moment. We must know God,
love God and depend on Him for what lies ahead. Hear
the word of Jesus, and we will go to the next thoughts
concerning love. His time was approaching, and He told
His disciples:

*"Behold, the hour cometh, yea, is now come,
that ye shall be scattered, every man to his own,
and shall leave me alone: and yet I am not
alone, because the Father is with me. These
things I have spoken unto you, that in me ye
might have peace. In the world ye shall have
tribulation: but be of good cheer; I have overcome the world" (John 16:32-33).*

Shortly before this time He told them:

*"Peace I leave with you, my peace I give unto
you; not as the world giveth, give I unto you. Let
not your heart be troubled, neither let it be
afraid" (John 14:27).*

Peace, untroubled hearts: can we in our greatest illusory
dreams think of anything in our lives that would be better than to have peace and be without concern for what

19

is before us? It is so easily attainable, all we need do is love God, have faith in His promises and do as He asks of us. We are not speaking of the outward being but that peace and tranquility that is in our inner being, the only place it will be found and be effective.

CHAPTER 4

In the Gospel of Luke, there is an interesting story which we will review, and it will introduce us to the next consideration in our study of love. Jesus is narrator of the story, and He tells of a man travelling from Jerusalem to Jericho who fell among thieves. He was stripped of his clothing, wounded and left lying in the road half dead. We have no further information about the man, whether he was Jew or Gentile, if he was a ranking citizen of a certain place, his lineage, or even if he was a religious man. Of course, as far as Jesus' parable is concerned, these are of little consequence. Jesus was teaching a lesson. The route he was traveling, according to secular history, was a twenty-one mile stretch of very rugged and rocky terrain which would lend itself for the hiding of thieves and other sorts of criminals.

By chance, a priest happened by and saw the wounded man and passed by on the other side. Following this, a Levite was there, looked at the man and passed by on the other side. (The Levite was of the priestly tribe descended from Levi who were set apart to serve God. The Levites assisted the priests in their service and were also temple guards.) So, two so-called men of God saw a man in need but went past him on the other side of the road. Hardly what we would expect from priests and temple workers. The priest was duty-bound to help this man in need, but he refused to do so.

The Levite also had an obligation to be of help but instead looked and went on his way. Evidently, both chose to ignore the man in need, probably didn't want to go to the trouble and expense of being helpful. One totally ignored the man, the other looked and went on his way: no concern, no compassion, no help, not even a cloak or coat to cover the man to protect him from the elements, they were likely fearful of getting involved with the robbers themselves. Whatever their reasoning, they could not justify their action or lack thereof. As we take a moment to ponder this, we realize it is not so different from the attitudes of so many of our fellowman in today's world. Selfishness, greed, stinginess, and lack of concern are very much prevalent in our world. But let's move on with the story. Jesus continues.

A man from Samaria was also journeying the same road. He saw the man and had compassion on him. He went to him, bound his wounds, anointed him with oil and wine and set him on his own animal and took him to an inn. This is what should have taken place with one or the other who first saw him. The injured man was likely a Jew, this person was a Samaritan. Jews and Samaritans did not mingle, the Jews hated the Samaritans, yet he ignored the fact that he also could be accosted by the crooks. He had compassion and did what was neighborly even though they were not likely neighbors. He stayed the night, and when he went on his way, he left money for the care of the man. More than that, he pledged to return and satisfy any other expenses incurred. Then Jesus makes his point: "Which now of these three, thinkest thou, was neighbor unto him that fell among the thieves?" The answer would have been evident; the one who had mercy. Read the account in Luke 10:30-36.

Jesus made it known as he spoke to the multitudes that those who were merciful will be rewarded with mercy (Matthew 5:7). Shortly thereafter, He said:

> *"Ye have heard that it hath been said, Thou shalt love thy neighbor, and hate thine enemy. But I say unto you, love your enemies, bless them that curse you, do good to them that hate you, and pray for them that despitefully use you, and persecute you" (Matthew 5:43-44).*

We are in the process of making an examination of the subject of love and look what Jesus has just told us. We are to love our enemies. To love our neighbor is easier to fulfill. Generally, we get along with our neighbors, but Jesus wasn't talking about getting along, being agreeable, speaking, helping when in need, no: He said we are to love our neighbor, and we are to have the same love for our enemies. That is a large undertaking.

Jesus didn't use the word *Phileo,* which is not as strong a word in meaning as *Agape,* which He did use when He said love your enemy. There is no question as to what was intended. If your enemy despises you, we still are to love that enemy, seek the highest good, be compassionate, be charitable. Not an easy task, but it is what Jesus expects of us. Neither He nor His word ever taught hatred. We have been taught to hate sin and evil ways but not to hate the sinner. The word translated here as hate means to love less and is not as strong as the word for hate in KJV. Nonetheless, we are not dealing in Greek meanings as much as we are hearing the lesson that our Lord wants us to fully understand. We are to hate nobody, we are to love our neighbor, our fellow-man as we love ourselves (Matthew 19:19). This was taught to the Jews back in the days of Moses (Leviticus 19:18).

The Apostle John gives us record of Jesus' words:

"A new commandment I give unto you, That ye love one another; even as I have loved you, that ye also love one another, by this shall all men know that ye are my disciples if ye have love one to another" (John 13:34-35).

Jesus is speaking of the ultimate meaning of love when He says, "as I have loved you." Think about this for a moment. His love could not be surpassed in any manner. He was in heaven with the Father, it was Him through whom all of creation came to be, and His love was so great that He would leave heaven and come to earth, live in poverty and danger, and finally suffer the brutal beatings and the cruel death on the cross to provide salvation for a sinful world. The commandment for love is not new, but this kind of love shown by the Savior is the ultimate expression of love.

> *"This is my commandment, That ye love one another, as I have loved you. Greater love hath no man than this, that a man lay down his life for his friends" (John 15:12-13).*

It was not to be long before Jesus lay down His life for all of mankind. This was love at its Zenith, the high point, the greatest expression of love possible. Jesus said: "Ye are my friends if ye do whatsoever I command you" (vs. 14). This is the standard that Jesus has set for us to follow. We will never achieve love for our fellow-man to that extent, but we certainly can heed His teaching to the best of our ability. His will is that we love one another, and we can surely strive to reach that goal.

Paul wrote to the church in Rome. "Be kindly affectioned one to another with brotherly love, in honor preferring one another" (Romans 12:10). Seems easy enough, doesn't it? Love each other with brotherly affection and be happy to honor each other. He was writing primarily to Christians, but it certainly does not negate our showing love for all mankind, remember He said your neighbor <u>and</u> your enemy. Jesus said:

> *"For if ye love them which love you, what thank have ye? For sinners also love those that love them... But love ye your enemies, and do good, and lend, hoping for nothing again; and your*

reward shall be great, and ye shall be the children of the Highest: for He is kind unto the unthankful and to the evil" (Luke 6:32, 35).

This is the pattern that Jesus has set for us; we will do well if we do our best to comply to His wishes. To the Ephesians, Paul wrote:

"Walk in love, as Christ also hath loved us, and hath given himself for us an offering and a sacrifice to God for a sweetsmelling savor" (Ephesians 5:2).

God was pleased with Christ for fulfilling His wishes; in the same manner, we should be full of love for others. To do as Jesus asks would create a totally different world than the present. He said our love should come from a pure heart and be given freely. James referred to this as the royal law: "If ye fulfill the royal law according to the scripture, thou shalt love thy neighbor as thy self, ye do well" (James 2:8).

CHAPTER 5

Jesus said:

"He that hath my commandments, and keepeth them, he it is that loveth me; and he that loveth me shall be loved by my Father, and I will love him, and will manifest myself to him" (John 14:21).

Jesus was not inclined to issue a challenge as such, but He did lay out in no uncertain terms what is going to be expected. To say that love is a religious duty would not be incorrect; love is a religious duty to those who choose to honor God and to abide by his will. However, beyond being a religious responsibility, it is one also that pertains to our manner of living in the world. Love covers such a sweeping range of intent and emotion that we could not limit it in any one area. So far in this writing, we have covered many thoughts and truths about the meaning and usage of the word love, it would be folly to attempt to limit it only as a religious practice. We do not question any of Christ's teaching. If we keep His commandments, it is a promise, He will love us and manifest himself to us. We have evidence of this every day of our life. We see Him in all the beautiful blessings we receive every day, He is keeping the promise made to those who are doing His will.

Before we finish this writing, we will have more to consider about God's blessings. However, there are many other blessings that mankind is sharing simply because God has made it so. We are talking about temporal or physical blessings that all may enjoy. All the *spiritual* blessings are limited to those who love God and abide by His commandments. The temporal blessings He has made to be used by all, but it is because He loves mankind and is hopeful that all will become obedient to His will for man. Jesus pointed out when He was teaching on the mountain, "He maketh His sun to rise on the evil and on the good, and sendeth rain on the just and on the unjust" (Matthew 5:45). It is because of God's love that all will receive these blessings. God makes no difference in blessings such as this, He is a benevolent God. Also, it is a continuation of the lesson on loving all, even those who do not love us or our enemies. We need to take this message and do as God would have us do, as we have seen, love our fellow man whatever the circumstances.

What are some of the temporal blessings we likely need to be reminded of if we are not a follower of God? Let's begin with what is or should be the most meaningful blessing that is universal. Our spouse and children: what a wonderful addition to our lives. The joy of having a home and sharing our life with a family. This is a blessing available to any who choose to make it so. Another would be our means of providing for that family, to have a job in which we can be productive, happy and care for our loved ones. Let's step outside the door and view the magnificence of all that God has created. The flora and fauna of nature that is indigenous in our part of the world, wherever that might be: another part of God's creation for the benefit all. We can be amazed by peering into the night's majestic display of the Lord's handiwork. The billions of stars in the Milky Way alone, the moon He created to light the night sky, to catch a glimpse of a comet as it whirls through the darkness. God has provided the soil to grow our food and the rain that falls to sustain the growth, and the technology to develop and manufacture the needs of continuing life support. We could continue to name the universal blessings, but this is sufficient to help us understand the divine functioning of God's supplying the needs of mankind.

Because of God's love and mercy, He has made available to all of the world, who choose to make use of them, these universal blessings. He created man, and He has made a way for man to sustain himself with the means He gave to each to build a good and happy life. However, these blessings mentioned are just the basics, there are innumerable spiritual blessings of which God hopes we will avail ourselves. We will consider these a bit later. For now, there are some other areas to which we need to give thought to the all-embracing subject of love.

CHAPTER 6

As the Lord was speaking to Moses, recorded in the nineteenth chapter of Leviticus, He told him to teach certain things to the Israelites. One of the commandments he wished to be observed is in verse eighteen. "Thou shalt not avenge, nor bear any grudge against the children of thy people, but thou shalt love thy neighbor as thyself: I am Lord." It seems to be human nature to want revenge on those who have done wrong by us; God didn't want it to be so. We tend to hold grudges for real or assumed slights; God says that is not the way to live. He said what He wanted is for all human beings to love others in the same manner one would love himself.

Peter had this to say about love: "And above all things have fervent love for one another, for love will cover a multitude of sins" (1 Peter 4:8, NKJV). He had admonished Christians not to be neglectful of prayer and be serious about it; what was important is to show deep love for each other; love would make up for many faults.

Jesus was near the end of His earthly ministry and was wanting to be certain that the Apostles would be unified in their work. They were to love each other as He loved them, and He in fact addressed this again, "This my commandment, that ye love one another as I have loved you" (John 15:12). We have earlier talked about the depth of Christ's love. To love as He did was a meaningful command.

Paul reminded Christians:

"But concerning brotherly love you have no need that I should write to you, for you yourselves were taught by God to love one another" *(1 Thessalonians 4:9, NKJV).*

Do not forget that Jesus said we are to love our enemies the same way. John did not fail to address this issue:

"And this is His commandment, that we should believe on the name of His Son Jesus, and love one another, as He gave us commandment" *(1 John 3:23).*

And this is what God says we must do, there is no escape clause in the writing. Here is another thought from John:

"And we have known and believe the love that God hath to us. God is love; and he that dwelleth in love dwelleth in God, and God in him" *(1 John 4:16).*

This is the key to being prepared to fulfil this commandment of love. It must begin with faith in the fact that God does love us and lives within us and we in Him. John said: "And hereby we do know that we know Him, if we keep His commandments" (1 John 2:4). "But whoso keepeth his word, in Him verily is the love of

God perfected" (vs. 5). Jesus said "if ye know these things, blessed are ye if you do them" (John 13:17). What we need to recognize and abide by is that these commands are not suggestions. It is incumbent on those choosing to do God's will to accept the responsibility of doing what He says.

Approaching this from the human standpoint, it is difficult to love our enemies, do good to those who hate us, bless those who curse us, despitefully use us and any who persecute us. In any of these situations, our first mortal impulse would be to "get even with them" or "I'll show 'em, they can't do me that way, I'll make 'em pay." This does not express love; it is more akin to hatred, and this should never be a part of our life for any reason. It is damaging to us and is unacceptable to God. Paul wrote to the Romans:

> *"If it be possible, as much as lieth in you, live peaceably with all men. Dearly beloved, avenge not yourselves, but rather give place unto wrath: for it is written, vengeance is mine; I will repay, saith the Lord. Therefore, if thine enemy hunger, feed him; if he thirsts give him drink; for in so doing thou shalt heap coals of fire on his head. Be not overcome with evil but overcome evil with good" (Romans 12:18-21).*

So, when our first impulse is to return evil for evil, stop, and remember what the Lord expects of us. As we noted earlier, it is not an easy thing to accomplish, but we need to make it an integral facet of our daily living.

32

Practice this always, and it will become an automatic and righteous way in our life. We will live a much happier life, and our Father will be happy also. Paul wrote:

"Fulfil ye my joy, that ye be likeminded, having the same love, being of one accord, of one mind. Let nothing be done through strife or vainglory; but in lowliness of mind let each esteem other better than themselves. Look not every man on his own things, but every man also on the things of others" (Philippians 2:3-4).

Once more the words of the Apostle Paul:

"Love suffers long and is kind; love does not envy; love does not parade itself, is not puffed up; does not behave rudely, does not seek its own, is not provoked, thinks no evil" (1 Corinthians 13:4-5, NKJV).

When we accept these truths, we are beginning to know what God expects from us.

Let's cover one more area of which we need to speak and then we will move on. We have in this chapter discussed the necessity of loving our fellow man, our neighbor, and our enemy. We have acceded to the fact that we must be in harmony with Bible teaching if we expect to be as God wishes us to be. So, if we are to exhibit an authentic, true love for all mankind we must have three attributes which will compel us to deal with our fellow man in the right manner.

Let's begin with faith; faith is belief, trust, conviction. We are going to have to be honest with ourselves. Jesus has given His instruction. When He says we are to love our enemy, do we intend to act accordingly? It will be seen in our life and our actions. It is what God wants from us, action and not lip service. We expect Jesus to fulfill His promises. He expects us to deal with our fellow man honestly and justly as faithful Christians. It is choosing to do the right thing. Function or failure: there is no middle ground. Faith without action is dead; we dare not lie to ourselves and get caught in the trap of doing nothing. James tells us that faith without works is dead. Faith is the beginning point; we proceed from there in our service to the Lord. If we intend to bake bread, we gather all the ingredients and begin the process, but until we add the yeast, nothing is going to happen; it would just be inert ingredients with no place to go. It is the same with fulfilling our responsibilities to God and our fellow man. We can prepare for the job ahead, but until we mix in faith, nothing is going to be accomplished.

Coupled with our faith, we will need enthusiasm. Without enthusiasm, we will never accomplish anything worthwhile. Christians have been fortunate in our knowing God's will and believing that Jesus is the Christ the Son of God. We have made ourselves partakers of His saving grace. We became Christians because we can know those who believe and obey His will are going to be with God for all of eternity. We have learned that those who are not in God's family will not have this privilege; eternity for those means unending misery and suffering. This is the reason we should be enthusiastic about how we deal with our fellowman. We do not wish that any should fail to become children of God, so we become inspired to share the gospel with others; this is part of our responsibility and compels us to fulfill our obligation to love all and deal fairly with everyone. Loving our fellowman and being concerned with his eternal well-being as our own, we will eagerly become teachers and leaders by the way we conduct our life. When we are fully convinced there is a heaven and a hell, why would we not want others to know this as well? Twice Paul spoke to the Corinthians about their zeal, their vehement desire to continue in their work in the church after his writing to them. This is what enthu-siasm amounts to, zeal, ardor, desire, passion, exuber-ance, when it comes to achieving our needs and acting on the commands of the Lord. Paul wrote of Epaphras in the letter to the Colossians about his zeal for the church at Colossae. Haphazard and purposeless atten-tion to duty will never suffice.

The third trait we should mention is communication. It is obvious that without communication nothing is go-ing to be disseminated. The finest example of the need for this we have seen in our Lord. He talked often with the Father in heaven. Having this example, it would be reasonable to believe that our first and foremost com-munication should be with God. Whatever Jesus was doing, He was in prayer talking to His Father. In this, He received guidance, strength, help, encouragement and miraculous abilities to further His teaching. We as God's family have the same privilege of being in communication with God through prayer. We can receive the same, other than miraculous power, when we pray and ask God.

Beyond that we cannot fulfill our responsibilities in teaching others without the benefit of communication. We fit ourselves for this by our study of the Bible and in putting this knowledge to work by talking with others. Another means of our being able to communicate is by what people see in us. This could possibly be one of the best methods of teaching for some. We are not all equipped with the same capabilities, some preach, some teach, others write and then there is always the lesson which comes from our conduct, the way we live our life. We spoke of this earlier, that was Christ's lesson in His sermon on the mount. We are the city on the hill, we are the lamp that shines and brings glory to the Father and leads people to Christ. Not counting Jesus, the Apostle Paul is the greatest, most effective teacher and example of enthusiasm in the history of the church. With all his preaching and teaching in his travels and all the correspondence with the churches by letter, he is probably the most prodigious and most successful communicator of all time.

CHAPTER 7

Up to this point, we have covered several areas of great importance as we are making this study of the subject of love and life. Of course, there is no area of the study of God's word that is not of great importance. However, in this writing, we have endeavored to focus our thoughts on this divinely inspired subject to enlighten each of us to what love is and clearly define its purpose in life, how we are to enmesh ourselves to true love and to manage our lives; accordingly, or perhaps simply to refresh our previous studies of this subject of love.

Whichever is the case, we need to pursue several other thoughts before we bring this to a close. One trying to complete an article, or end a book, or call a painting finished is always challenged with the feeling that there surely must be more to add. Some years ago, baseball great Yogi Berra coined the phrase, "it ain't over til it's over." How fitting, and in this case, we do need to add more thoughts which will be beneficial to completing our study. We have considered much about love so let's merge this study with thoughts about how we are to live on earth if we wish to live in heaven. This is where God wants us to be; are we in agreement with Him?

As we mentioned earlier in the writing, if it wasn't for love, there would be no world, but God's plan for mankind was born of love. Every good thing that we have experienced in our lifetime is the result of God's love. That is not only true in this lifetime on earth but projected all the way to the final phase of life which we understand to be an eternity, never ending. Wherever the pathway of life takes us, the challenges we face, the oppression, the worries, the successes, the highs, the lows make us understand the vicissitudes of life are ever present. But there is a protectant force that is changeless in which each of us, whatever is thrust our way, can entrust our lives; that is Jesus Christ. He is the same yesterday, today, and forever (Hebrews 13:8). James reminds us:

"Every good gift and every perfect gift is from above, and cometh down from the Father of lights, with whom is no variableness, neither shadow of turning" (James 1:17).

That greatest gift, the perfect gift is Jesus Christ our Savior who brought salvation from sin to all who will accept it. This must be the focal point of our life, accepting this precious gift and dedicating our time on earth to prepare for eternity. God's love and mercy brought this gift to us, and because He is the only pathway to eternity in heaven, we must be dedicated to living righteously and preparing for heaven. We cannot ignore this love and mercy and expect God to be happy with us. If we are to be found worthy of heaven, it will be because

38

we chose to accept the gift and do His bidding, by loving God and all of mankind. Centuries ago, Solomon had this to say:

"Trust in the Lord with all thine heart; and lean not upon thine own understanding. In all thy ways acknowledge Him, and He shall direct thy paths" (Proverbs 3:5-6).

Solomon was a very wise man, who better to listen to for safe guidance? Many years ago Jeremiah said: "The faithful love of the Lord never ends! His mercies never cease. Great is His faithfulness; His mercies begin afresh each morning" (Lamentations 3:22-23, NLT). What a testimony to the never-ending love and mercy of our God. It is astonishing when we attempt to grasp the depth of His love for man. It is not something due to us, it is not deserved, yet freely given. God said He would never forsake us; this is proof that no matter how undeserving we are His mercy fills our life constantly. A truth we need to think about; it is so real, and it is only because of God's mercy that we have an opportunity to prepare for eternity. Sin has so often separated us from God, but He has been merciful to all of us.

In today's world, there are too many distractions that capture our thoughts and desires. Because of this, we are in danger of losing sight of the fact that our reason for existence is not to satisfy our yearnings for worldly "things" but to devote our time and efforts for preparing to stand before Christ at the time of judgment. Lest we forget, the writer of the Hebrew letter pointed out that "It is appointed unto men once to die, but after this the judgment" (Hebrews 9:27). The author of the letter didn't put this in the text to fill up space; it is a dire warning. Whatever your thoughts might be makes no difference, there *will* be a time of judgment, we *will* each give an accounting of our lives and then the decision *will* be forthcoming. We will be in heaven for eternity, or we will be suffering in hell forever. There is no reason to soften the language; it is just plain fact stated for us to realize we are here to prepare for the future. John wrote:

> *"Love not the world, neither the things that are in the world, if any man love the world, the love of the Father is not in him. For all that is in the world, the lust of the flesh, and the lust of the eyes, and the pride of life, is not of the Father, but is of the world. And the world passeth away, and the lust thereof: but he that doeth the will of God abideth forever" (1 John 2:15-17).*

This fact is difficult for some to grasp. For many, it is easy to put God aside and strive with all our being to achieve the trinkets of the world, which as we noted before, these worldly goals are fleeting at best; the time will come when they will mean absolutely nothing, they will be worthless. Jesus put it succinctly in the sermon on the mount:

> *"No man can serve two masters: for you will hate one and love the other; you will be devoted*

to one and despise the other. You cannot serve both God and money" (Matthew 6:24, NLT).

Paul cautioned Timothy:

"Charge them that are rich in this world, that they be not highminded, nor trust in uncertain riches, but in the living God, who giveth us richly all things to enjoy" (1 Timothy 6:17).

The young ruler that approached Jesus, asking what he needed to do to be saved, was saddened when Jesus told him what he must do. Divest himself of his riches, give to the poor, and take up the cross and follow Jesus. And he was sad at that saying, and went away grieved: for he had great possessions (Mark 10:17-22). This is most likely one of the prime reasons people do not wish to follow Jesus and do His bidding; our worldly idols are too important to us. John said: "Little children, keep yourselves from idols" (1 John 5:21). We often lose sight of the fact that these things will one day be of no value whatsoever. This is what Paul was telling Timothy; admonish Christians not to be proud and trust in money or things, but their trust should be in the living God that supplies our needs.

Reading these scriptures forces us to understand that being blessed with eternal life in the presence of our God will not be obtained by worldly treasure. Peter wrote:

"For you know that God paid a ransom to save you from the empty life inherited from your ancestors. And the ransom He paid was not mere gold or silver. It was the precious blood of Christ, the sinless, spotless Lamb of God" (1 Peter 1:18-19, NLT).

So, that rules out anything temporal; there must be something else that is important for us to know and pursue. Jesus said that if one wants to be in heaven with the Father, it would be through Him. "I am the way, the truth, and the life: no man cometh unto the Father, but by me" (John 14:6). Jesus said it, there is no reason for any to question the fact—He is the only way to the Father and eternal life. Peter told the people in Jerusalem on Pentecost, as the gospel was preached for the first time, they had crucified Christ the Son of God. But God has raised Him up and they needed to know: "Neither is there salvation in any other: for there is none other name under heaven given among men, whereby we must be saved" (Acts 4:12).

So, this being an absolute; for us to continue our pursuit of salvation, we must depend on Jesus to tell us what we have to do. Jesus being the only way also rules out any teaching that is not in keeping with the instruction of the Bible which is given to us by God through the Holy Spirit. The Apostles were aware that man was attempting to add their thoughts to the scriptures, they would ignore any teaching they didn't like, so their warning was for all to be cautious about what they accepted as God's word. Paul admonished Timothy:

"For the time is coming when people will no longer listen to sound and wholesome teaching. They will follow their own desires and will look for teachers who will tell them whatever their itching ears want to hear. They will reject the truth and chase after myths" (2 Timothy 4:3-4, NLT).

Well that certainly clears up a lot of misunderstanding, doesn't it? Jesus said there is only one way to the Father; the world says there are hundreds of different ways. Who do we think we should believe; what the Lord says is right, or what man says: anything is okay? One doesn't have to have a doctorate in Quantum Physics to answer that question.

These thoughts bring up another thing we need to think about. Before Jesus ascended to heaven to be with the Father, He said He would return and at that time there would be a judgment and decisions about our eternal habitat. That was almost two thousand years ago. Should this cause us to think about how much time we will have to decide about accepting the teaching of the Bible or the ideas of man? Paul to the Romans:

"And that, knowing the time, that now it is high time to awake out of sleep: for now is our salvation nearer than when we believed. The night is far spent, the day is at hand: let us therefore

cast off the works of darkness and let us put on the armor of light. Let us walk honestly as in the day; not in rioting and drunkenness, not in chambering and wantonness, not in strife and envying. But put ye on the Lord Jesus Christ, and make not provision for the flesh, to fulfill the lusts thereof" (Romans 13:11-14).

What is Paul saying to us? Much time has passed since the Lord said He would return. Time perhaps is short, and we should wake up and face reality. The coming of the Lord is almost two thousand years closer than when He first announced it. Don't live the profligate life, live right and prepare for His coming. Do you know when Jesus is going to return? Certainly not. Do you believe you are ready to face Him at the judgment? Only you can answer that. Think about it and be certain of where you stand.

Taking into consideration everything we have covered up to this point, it is a good idea to pursue these thoughts and others that are pertinent, so we can make an intelligent assessment of our position with the Lord. It is extremely important that we do so. It is imperative that we have made the decisions which will put us in the correct relationship with God, and if we have not, we need to make corrections in our course before it is too late.

CHAPTER 8

In our lifetime on earth, we will face many challenges, we make decisions that are pertinent to our life and our future. There is no decision we will ever be called upon to make that is of greater importance than the decision we must make about where we will choose to live in eternity. Please do not brush past this without considering the statement. Someday each of us will run out of time in this physical life. Beyond the veil of this life lies eternity; we will then be in the final place of abode; forever, I repeat forever, forever. The final place of abode will be in heaven in the presence of our God for the saved. For those who have chosen to ignore God and His wishes, the final place of abode will be eternal suffering. God allows us to make the decision about where we will be for eternity. That is the reason for not ignoring the statement about being fully aware of the consequence of our choice: heaven or hell. It's our decision.

Since this is true, and we know it is because that's what the Bible teaches, so there can be no mistake; let's give some thought about our actions in the future.

Luke tells us in Acts 11:26 that the disciples were first called Christians in Antioch of Syria. These so named were those who had been convinced that Jesus was the Son of God. He had come to earth to sacrifice his life in order that sinners could be cleansed of sin, they confessed their belief and were then baptized for the ridding of sin and were added to the church which is the Body of Christ. This happened about 41 CE. They were named thus because they had become children of God by Christ's cleansing blood. Almost two thousand years ago, their obedience to Christ's teaching, and that alone, made them Christians. If this is the truth (and it is, it is what the Bible teaches), would there be any reason to think anything other than this would make Christians today? Ponder that thought a bit as we think about some other pertinent teaching from God's word.

Let's go back and think of Paul's word to the Romans, which we mentioned just a bit ago. Time is running out, the coming of the Lord is nearer than when we first knew of the Lord Jesus. He said the night is far gone, meaning a bit of the preparation time is already used up. We have no idea when the time will be up. If God had wanted us to know, He would have included it in the Bible. However, there is one thing that we do know; Peter warned us:

> *"But the day of the Lord will come as a thief in the night; in the which the heavens shall pass away with a great noise, and the elements shall melt with fervent heat, the earth also and the works that are therein shall be burned up" (2 Peter 3:10).*

Jesus said: "Watch therefore, for ye know neither the day nor the hour where in the Son of man cometh" (Matthew 25:13). Paul reminded the Thessalonians: "For yourselves know perfectly that the day of the Lord so cometh as a thief in the night" (1 Thessalonians 5:2). There are other scriptures that tell us the same thing, but this is enough to cause us to be vitally concerned about the lives we are living and if we are truly preparing ourselves to meet the Lord.

The day of the Lord is the day that Jesus returns, appearing in the clouds when He will be raising the dead and beginning the judgment.

> *"Marvel not at this: for the hour is coming, in the which all that are in the graves shall hear His voice, and shall come forth; they that have done good, unto the resurrection of life; and they that have done evil, unto the resurrection of damnation" (John 5:28-29).*

He is talking of the suddenness, being at a time when it is not expected. Knowing this and realizing that when that time comes there will be no more time to prepare, it will then be too late to make any difference. This being the case, it would be helpful now for us to consider some thoughts about truly being prepared to meet the Lord.

CHAPTER 9

We referred to the words of Jesus a bit earlier. He said: "I am the way, the truth, and the life: no man cometh unto the Father, but by me." This leaves no room for doubt or question. If we see God in heaven, it will be because we have put on Christ by baptism, as we have studied a while back. Paul told the Galatians:

"Yet we know that a person is made right with God by faith in Jesus Christ, not by obeying the law. And we have believed in Christ Jesus, so that we might be made right with God because of our faith in Christ, not because we have obeyed the law. For no one will ever be made right with God by obeying the law" (Galatians 2:16, NLT).

There was another message in this passage of scripture, but here we are concerned about being in Christ and cleansed from sin. Paul wrote to the Romans:

"Don't you realize that you become the slave of whatever you choose to obey? You can be a slave, which leads to death, or you can choose to obey God, which leads to righteous living. Thank God! Once you were slaves of sin, but now you wholeheartedly obey this teaching we have given you. Now you are free from your slavery to sin, and you have become slaves to righteousness" (Romans 6:16-18, NLT).

We are cleansed and made free from sin by the blood of Christ (Ephesians 2:13). "For ye are all the children of God by faith in Christ Jesus. For as many of you as have been baptized into Christ have put on Christ" (Galatians 3:26-27). Now it is imperative that we remain sin free.

> *"Know ye not that the unrighteous shall not inherit the kingdom of God? Be not deceived: neither fornicators, nor idolaters, nor adulterers, nor effeminate, nor abusers of themselves with mankind, nor thieves, nor covetous, nor drunkards, nor revilers, nor extortioners, shall inherit the kingdom of God" (1 Corinthians 6:9-10).*

Paul said some of them had been doing these things, but now they were cleansed. And we must guard against sin as best we can. Satan's greatest joy comes from seeing a child of God drawn away from righteousness into sin. James warned:

> *"But every man is tempted, when he is drawn away of his own lust, and enticed. Then when lust hath conceived, it bringeth forth sin: and sin, when it is finished bringeth forth death" (James 1:14-15).*

The words of Paul:

> *"Dear brothers and sisters pattern your lives after mine and learn from those who follow our example. For I have told you often before, and I say it again with tears in my eyes, that there are*

many whose conduct shows they are really ene-mies of the cross of Christ. They are headed for destruction. Their God is their appetite, they brag about shameful things, and they think only about this life here on earth. But we are citizens of heaven, where the Lord Jesus Christ lives. And we are eagerly waiting for him to return as our savior" (Philippians 3:17-20, NLT).

We know God does not want anyone to be lost, but we also know that He is no respecter of persons, we will be judged by what our lives have or have not been.

"Knowing that of the Lord ye shall receive the reward of inheritance: for ye serve the Lord Christ. But he that doeth wrong shall receive for the wrong which he hath done: and there is no respect of persons" (Colossians 3:24-25).

Peter gives us something to ponder:

"For the time has come for judgment, and it must begin with God's household. And if judg-ment begins with us, what terrible fate awaits those who have never obeyed God's good news? ...if the righteous are barely saved what will happen to godless sinners? (1 Peter 4:17-18, NLT).

We noted earlier in the writing that there is to be a time of judgment when Jesus returns to earth. Each of us will give an account of our lifetime.

"For it is written, As I live saith the Lord, every knee shall bow to me, and every tongue shall confess to God. So then every one of us shall give account of himself to God" (Romans 14:11-12).

There can be no doubt, we cannot misunderstand that simple fact. In that case then we must use our allotted time to prepare for that coming event. When the time of judgment comes, decisions will be made and verdicts announced.

"When the Son of man shall come in his glory, and all the holy angels with Him, then shall He sit upon the throne of his glory: and before Him shall be gathered all nations; and He shall separate them one from another, as a shepherd divideth his sheep from the goats: And He shall set the sheep on his right hand, but the goats on the left. Then shall the King say unto them on His right hand, Come, ye blessed of my Father, inherit the Kingdom prepared for you from the foundation of the world... Then shall he say also unto them on the left hand, depart from me, ye cursed, into everlasting fire, prepared for the devil and his angels" (Matthew 25:31-34, 41).

That is all, there are no alternatives from which to choose, no middle ground, no fence sitting, a simple choice: heaven or hell.

CHAPTER 10

There is no higher calling in this lifetime, no title or recognition that will ever mean as much as being a Christian. As we have pointed out previously, there is no accomplishment, no fulfillment of our wishes and needs that will ever be as significant as being a child of God. Everything that touches our lives temporally as we make our way toward the final phase of eternity will in the end be of no importance at all. We just read about what is going to happen to the world and everything that is in the world when Jesus decides to come again. Knowing without question that these facts are true and are supported by the text, let's go from here with some thoughts on how the Christian lives in preparation to meet the Lord.

The Apostle Paul was known for his tender love and kindness; it was so obvious in his writing. When he wrote to the church in Galatia, he was aware there were situations there which needed to be corrected. Souls were in danger of being lost because of false teachers. However, there would be no question left when he told them firmly how to correct the situations. Listen to his opening words of that letter.

"Grace be to you and peace from God the Father, and from our Lord Jesus Christ, who gave Himself for our sins, that He might deliver us

from this present evil world according to the will of God our Father: To whom be glory for ever and ever" (Galatians 1:3-5).

He indicated his love and concern for the people. He bid that God's and Christ's love and peace be with them. This was pretty much the way he opened each of his letters. His letters to the various churches were always letters of love and concern for the Christians to whom he was writing. He could be tender, and he could be firm if called for, whatever was needed to help them to live right because he was concerned with their eternal home. The gospel was quite new and different, and there were those who didn't fully understand, and those who deliberately attempted to lead followers into error. He did not wish to see any child of God fail by ignoring the instructions they had that caused them to become Christians, or fail because they were not living as the Word of God instructed. In his letter to the churches of Ephesus, he reminded them of the blessings which came to those in Christ.

"May God our Father and the Lord Jesus Christ give you grace and peace. All praise to God, the Father of our Lord Jesus Christ, who has blessed us with every spiritual blessing in the heavenly realms because we are united with Christ" (Ephesians 1:2-3, NLT).

He also would remind those in the Kingdom that they had not always enjoyed the blessings of God's family. He wrote of the times before they learned the truth and were baptized into Christ.

> *"In those days you were living apart from Christ. You were excluded from citizenship among the people of Israel, and you did not know the covenant promises God had made to them. You lived in this world without God and without hope. But now you have been united with Christ Jesus. Once you were far away from God, but now you have been brought near to Him through the blood of Christ" (Ephesians 2:12-13, NLT).*

So, it is evident that drastic changes are made in one's life when one takes hold of the Salvation from sin and the promise of eternal life which will be the reward of the faithful. This is what Paul was emphasizing when he wrote to the Corinthians.

> *"Therefore, if any man be in Christ, he is a new creature: old things are passed away; behold, all things are become new" (2 Corinthians 5:17).*

Also, to the Colossians:

> *"Don't lie to each other, for you have stripped off your old sinful nature and all its wicked deeds. Put on your new nature and be renewed as you learn to know your Creator and become like Him" (Colossians 3:9-10, NLT).*

We understand that now the old life we lived is gone, and there is a new life for us to use in preparation. As we mentioned earlier, we are made new in our obedience to the will of Christ. We are new because we have put on Christ. Paul wrote to the Romans:

"Know ye not, that so many of us as were baptized into Jesus Christ were baptized into His death? Therefore, we are buried with Him by baptism into death: that like as Christ was raised up from the dead by the glory of the Father, even so we should walk in newness of life" (Romans 6:3-4).

A bit later in the letter he told them how to begin to live as God's family.

"I beseech you therefore, brethren by the mercies of God, that ye present your bodies a living sacrifice, holy, acceptable unto God, which is your reasonable service. And be not conformed to this world: but be ye transformed by the renewing of your mind, that ye may prove what is that good, and acceptable, and perfect, will of God" (Romans 12:1-2).

The Lord is not asking for more than we are capable of. As much as we can, we must mimic Christ and His sacrifice. He was the perfect sacrifice. He gave His life, shed His blood so that all could be redeemed. For our way of life to be acceptable to Him, we must also make the sacrifice; giving ourselves to service in the Kingdom, shedding the sins of worldliness, dedicating ourselves to worshipping God and praising Him for the many blessings we receive. We must crucify the temporal desires for gadgets and idols of the world. The Christian takes upon himself the fruits of the spirit as Paul admonished the Galatians. To saturate our lives with these elements is to shield ourselves from being overcome with worldliness. These fruits will be better understood as attributes of our spiritual being. Paul said these are love, joy, peace, longsuffering, gentleness, goodness, faith, meekness, and temperance (Galatians 5:22-23a). These traits are a gift to the Christian and are the nucleus, the heart, of righteousness and the motivating force that prompts us, always going forward in our service, our dedication to Christ our Savior.

The Christian is endowed with so many blessings in this life; blessings which God chooses for us to make our lives better, but more meaningful than these are the spiritual blessings that the child of God receives. These blessings make our lives more closely attuned to God and are beneficial to a worthwhile life. Living righteously, helping us to be more Christ-like and doing all that we are able to do for our fellowman. Paul told the Romans:

"I myself also are persuaded of you, my brethren, that ye also are full of goodness, filled with all knowledge, able also to admonish one another" (Romans 15:14).

The reason we are so blessed is so we can be a blessing to others in our Christian walk. Spiritual gifts, like other strengths, blossom if we use them. Paul was reminding them that they need to be teaching and strengthening other Christians and those still outside of Christ.

Two more thoughts from Paul:

"Now we have received, not the spirit of the world, but the spirit which is of God; that we might know the things that are freely given to us of God. Which things also we speak, not in the words which man's wisdom teacheth, but which the Holy Spirit teacheth; comparing spiritual things with spiritual" (1 Corinthians 2:12-13).

Also:

"For our rejoicing is this, the testimony of our conscience, that in simplicity and godly sincerity, not with fleshly wisdom, but by the grace of God, we have had our life in the world, and more abundantly to you-ward" (2 Corinthians 1:12).

Teaching those truths of the Holy Spirit and not things of man, using the words of the Holy Spirit and not from those foisted by false teachers. Using these blessings means that God is working through us.

"For it is God which worketh in you both to will and to do of his good pleasure. Do all things without murmurings and disputings: That ye

may be blameless and harmless, the sons of God, without rebuke, in the midst of a crooked and perverse nation, among whom ye shine as lights in the world" (Philippians 2:13-15).

CHAPTER 11

Blessings, like love and mercy, are not something earned or due to us. They come to us freely from our Father. Gifts not to be hoarded within our being but to be shared, to be used to teach, for strength, to enrich our lives with the workings of the Holy Spirit within to spread happiness, peace, and the story of the gospel to others. Peter wrote:

"Grace and peace be multiplied unto you through the knowledge of God, and of Jesus our Lord, according as his divine power hath given unto us all things that pertain unto life and godliness, through the knowledge of him that hath called us to glory and virtue. Whereby are given unto us exceeding great and precious promises: that by these ye might be partakers of the divine nature, having escaped the corruption that is in the world through lust" (2 Peter 1:2-4).

The magnitude of these promises we understand to be far more than great and precious. How grand they are then, and how meaningful to each of us who will be partakers of the promises. Paul wrote:

"But as it is written, Eye hath not seen, nor ear heard, neither have entered into the heart of man, the things which God hath prepared for them that love Him" (1 Corinthians 2:9).

The most abundant and meaningful was the promise of the Savior, that through Him we may have life in eternity in the presence of the Father, the Son, and the Holy Spirit. What heaven will be is far beyond the imagination of our finite minds, but we can know assuredly that it will be a majestic home, and we will have fellowship with all the saved. That is a magnificent promise from our Savior Jesus Christ.

As the family of God, we have enjoyed the peace, tranquility, happiness in this life because of the blessings; these will be meager compared to the joy we will have when we receive that crown of life. What a colossal blessing this is; it is a gift from God in which we had no input. "For by grace are ye saved through faith; and that not of yourselves: it is the gift of God: not of works, lest any man should boast" Ephesians 2:8-9. It is by our faith in Jesus as God's Son and by God's love and grace we may obtain this wonderful blessing. We obtain this blessing by obeying Christ's instructions for salvation. Salvation is not a reward for the good we have done, so we take no credit for it.

About fifteen hundred years before Paul was writing these truths to the Ephesians, Moses was passing God's instruction to the Israelites.

"Now therefore if you will obey my voice indeed, and keep my covenant, then ye shall be a peculiar treasure unto me above all people" (Exodus 19:5).

60

This is the simple requirement from God; it is all that He and Jesus have asked from mankind. Believe God's word and obey the commandments, and we will benefit from the promises they have given us. When God asked the Israelites for obedience and they complied, they were rewarded with the promises made. When Jesus asks us for obedience to His will, we will be rewarded with eternal life. From Adam and Eve until the end of the earth, disobedience has had its cost. It will ever be so and if we are honest, we know that to be true and expect no less.

When Jesus said, "I am the way, the truth, and the life: no man cometh to the Father but by me"; when He said, "I am the resurrection and the life"; when He said. "I am come that they might have life"; when the prophet said that He would "save his people from their sins"; these were not idle words, these are the exceeding great and precious promises which we long to see fulfilled. We will see them pour out eternal life for those who keep the Lord's commandments. Just before Jesus returned to heaven, he told the apostles:

> *"Go ye into all the world, and preach the gospel to every creature. He that believeth and is baptized shall be saved; but he that believeth not shall be damned" (Mark 16:15-16).*

That is it: believe that Jesus is the Son of God and turn from the past life, confess that you believe and be baptized. This made Christians two thousand years ago; it is still making Christians in the present time. We live a righteous life as best we can, be penitent and ask for forgiveness when we fail, this is what Jesus wishes for us to follow. Live this way and be faithful to the end and we will be rewarded with a crown of life and an eternity with God and all the saved. This is another promise that Jesus made, hear His words:

> *"Don't let your hearts be troubled. Trust in God, and trust also in me. There is more than enough room in my father's home. If this were not so, would I have told you that I am going to prepare a place for you? When everything is ready, I will come and get you, so that you will always be with me where I am. And you shall know the way to where I am going" (John 14:1-4, NLT).*

These are comforting words that Jesus left with us. Can we envision anything that would be of greater value? Christ, God's Son, left the glorious heaven and the presence with His Father, to come to earth and dwell with the common man, became sin for all of mankind, sacrificed His life in order to provide eternal life for us; then, went back to prepare a place for us to be with Him in eternity?

How much love can one give for others? Jesus, by his life and death, made us realize what true love is. Jesus said:

> *"He that heareth my word, and believeth on Him that sent me, hath everlasting life, and*

shall not come into condemnation; but is passed from death into life" (John 5:24).

Now we fully understand the things God has prepared for us, what is meant by the exceeding great and precious promises. When we become Christians and are cleansed of sins, we understand it is talking about the spiritual blessings of this life and life in heaven for eternity. Also, it is free, we receive it because of God's love and His grace, not of men but of God. So, now we sit back and wait, we have nothing to do, no responsibilities, just rest easy and bask in the sunshine of God's love. No, that is not entirely correct. In fact, it is not even a little bit correct. It is true, salvation is free for all of mankind, but there are stipulations. Let's spend some time looking at some thoughts of which we need to be aware.

CHAPTER 12

We began chapter ten with this thought and wish to reiterate that truth for emphasis. There is no higher calling in this lifetime, no title or recognition that can mean as much as being a Christian. The name Christian is a holy name; it is a separating name because we are set apart. Peter termed it this way:

> *"But ye are a chosen generation, a royal priest-hood, an holy nation, a peculiar people; that ye should shew forth the praises of him who hath called you out of darkness into his marvelous light" (1 Peter 2:9).*

When we consider the lordly rank of those designations, they become very meaningful. This is not something we skip over lightly and then forget. It is very important that the Christian understands what they mean and how they are to be used. We are chosen, elected, because we have been brought to Christ by His gospel, thus a royal priesthood; charged with the responsibility and learning the capability of telling others of this splendid calling and the promises which belong to that Holy Nation, the kingdom of God and God is our King. All this makes a different kind of people; "peculiar" is the way Peter stated it. There are two kingdoms: the worldly kingdom out of which the Christian has been called and through obedience to Christ has been translated into the Holy Kingdom, that kingdom where the saved are dwelling, living righteous lives and spreading the good news of salvation through Jesus Christ. Paul said those who are saved and in Christ Jesus are saints. The only miracle involved with our becoming saints is the miracle of our Lord's death, burial and resurrection. So, we realize there is more to being a child of God than sitting and waiting for Jesus to return.

Having made the transition from the world to the kingdom of Christ, we are now a different people as Peter mentioned. Paul told the Colossians to set their affection on things above, not on things on the earth. "For ye are dead, and your life is hid with Christ in God" (Colossians 3:2-3). It goes without saying that if we are concerned about spiritual things, we have little time for the aggravation of this fallen world; our spiritual life is about heavenly things. Living in this mode we will devote more time to a prayer life, which is extremely important. Paul told the Ephesians:

"Praying always with all prayer and supplication in the Spirit, and watching thereunto with all perseverance and supplication for all saints" (Ephesians 6:18).

To the Thessalonians, Paul put it very simply: "Pray without ceasing" (1 Thessalonians 5:17). It is obvious that it is an impossibility to pray constantly day and night without stopping. Paul's intent was to tell them to be always in a prayerful spirit. This we can do. Being in a prayerful spirit always will eliminate straying off course, using unacceptable language, finding fault with our fellowman and being critical or jealous of others. Being in this attitude, we have a far greater tendency to treat others with love, grace and understanding which are critical attributes for the Christian. Let's hear more from the Apostle Paul:

> *"And let the peace of God rule in your hearts, to the which also you are called in one body; and be ye thankful. Let the word of Christ dwell in you richly in all wisdom; teaching and admonishing one another in psalms and hymns and spiritual songs, singing with grace in your hearts to the Lord. And whatsoever you do in Word or deed, do all in the name of the Lord Jesus, giving thanks to God and the Father by Him" (Colossians 3:15-17).*

If we struggle with these things, the Holy Spirit is always within us and is always helping us do what we wish to accomplish.

> *"Likewise the spirit also helpeth our infirmities: for we know not what we should pray for as we ought: but the Spirit itself maketh intercession for us with groanings which cannot be uttered. And He that searcheth the hearts knoweth what is the mind of the Spirit, because He maketh intercession for the saints according to the will of God" (Romans 8:26-27).*

What an added blessing to the child of God, the Holy Spirit dwelling within us is helping us in our prayers and guides us in our teaching of the gospel and comforts us in our time of need. All of this because of the love of our Father who wants us to live righteously, loving all our contemporaries and dedicate our lives to teaching the gospel of Christ to others in order that they too may have this hope of eternal life. As Paul said, our hope of glory is because Christ is in us (Colossians 1:27). Why is all of this important to us? Because God does not want any to perish and suffer eternally; He wants all to repent and become a part of the Kingdom of Christ.

Peter, in his first epistle, had admonishments for the Christian which we need to ponder and act upon. He reminded us of things which the child of God should treasure. In opening the letter, he prayed blessings on the church everywhere.

> *"Blessed be the God and Father of our Lord Jesus Christ, which according to his abundant mercy hath begotten us again unto a lively hope by the resurrection of Jesus Christ from the dead. To an inheritance incorruptible, and undefiled, and that fadeth not away, reserved in heaven for you who are kept by the power of God through faith unto salvation ready to be revealed in the last time" (1 Peter 1:3-5).*

A reminder of the most beautiful and meaningful blessing we can receive, eternal life in heaven with all the saints. He also spoke of needs for the Christians, so let's delve in a bit deeper.

CHAPTER 13

"Dear friends, I warn you as temporary resi-
dents and foreigners to keep away from worldly
desires that wage war against your very souls.
Be careful to live properly among your unbe-
lieving neighbors. Then even if they accuse you
of doing wrong, they will see your honorable
behavior, and they will give honor to God when
He judges the world" (1 Peter 2:11-12, NLT).

Peter says that we are not at home here on earth, we
are as strangers, our real home is in heaven, so it is imperative that we refrain from the evil pleasures of this
world. If we do this and live a good life, others will see
this; perhaps they too will glorify God. This a responsibility for all of God's family. Be the "city that is set on
the hill," be the "candle that is not hidden but put on the
candle stand that all may see," a needful responsibility
which we must show the world.

We are fully aware that our time on earth is limited,
we are passing this way on our journey to the final phase
of eternity. All the temporal things of this world will become as nothing, we can't let them separate us from
God. One bearing the banner of God's family but living
as the nephew of the devil will never lead anyone to
Christ, to say nothing of the result of his own failure. I
do not know the origin of the saying, "A hypocrite is
one who never intends to be what he pretends to be,"

but it fits well for some. If we choose to be unsavory citizens who are disreputable, shady, dishonest and offensive, we will not be serving God. The Philippians were reminded that our citizenship is in heaven, and we eagerly await a Savior from there, the Lord Jesus Christ. If this is correct, and we know it is, God said so, then we have little or no reason to be concerned with earthen treasures. We just need to live righteous lives in the presence of God.

Another important consideration to think about. We must have good morals by which we conduct our living. We must be honest, loving, caring, willing to help those in need, etc., but this alone is not enough for us to be satisfactory to God. When Jesus was being tempted in the wilderness, the devil tried to entice Him with worldly holdings if He would only worship the devil. Jesus told him: "Get thee behind me, Satan: for it is written, Thou shalt worship the Lord thy God, and Him only shalt thou serve" (Luke 4:8).

John, quoting Jesus, reminds us:

> *"But the hour cometh, and now is, when the true worshippers shall worship Him in spirit and in truth: for the Father seeketh such to worship Him. God is a Spirit: and they that worship Him must worship Him in spirit and in truth" (John 4:23-24).*

God expects us to worship Him, and why would we not be happy to do that? He is the creator of everything that exists, He is the source of every blessing we receive; it is He who sent Jesus to earth to be sacrificed to satisfy the debt of sin. We must acknowledge Him as the Sovereign God, and He deserves every deliberation about worshipping Him because of what He is and what He has done for us. This precludes pseudo-worship and half-way measures of recognizing Him as our heavenly Father. It also precludes our being remiss in assembling ourselves with other saints in the times set aside for this worship in congregant. Worshipping with the congregation is a time specified for that service. True worship goes much further than that. If we are to worship our God in Spirit, we must set aside other times for our personal appearance before Him to praise, glorify and worship Him. The writer of the Hebrew letter warned us about forsaking the assembling of ourselves together (Hebrews 10:25). The Apostles warned us about not being worshipful unto God in our daily living; we risk the dissatisfaction of our Father if we ignore them.

We glorify God in our assembly, and we are reminded by Jesus to celebrate His death and victory when He came to save His people from their sins. Christ suffered a brutal and cruel death when He was crucified for our sins. He did this willingly because God chose for Him to do so. He was victorious over all when He arose on the third day after being entombed. As He partook of His last meal with the apostles, He instituted the celebration, the memorial that is to remind each of us on the first day of every week to remember His death and what it accomplished: salvation for all who will accept it. If Jesus wanted us to have this communion service each Sunday, how dare we ignore it? He suffered a miserable six hours on the cross for us; can we not set aside time to praise Him and remember what it means to the child of God and how it came to be so.

According to Bible instruction every congregation of the Lord's church, His body, is autonomous. To put it simply, each congregation is responsible for its ongoing work. There are no headquarters, no organizations by which the congregation receives outside support, each is entirely self-supporting. There is no hierarchy to hand down edicts, laws and instruction. Each congregation appoints Elders, men who meet the guidelines to become an elder and are capable of being teachers and leaders in the church. They direct the activities of that particular congregation, they are set apart to serve, accepted by the congregation but are made overseers by the Holy Spirit (Acts 20:28).

"And when they had ordained themselves elders in every church, and prayed with fasting, they commended them to the Lord, on whom they believed" (Acts 14:23)

As the spiritual guides for the congregation, they determine when the congregation should meet and where. They work with the teachers to make sure they are grounded in truth and teach accordingly. They determine the times for worship service and counsel Christians on how each is to return to the Lord, His church, an acceptable amount of money which God provided. If we do not contribute to the work of the church, we are not fulfilling what is required. God blesses us so richly, why would we be stingy and greedy and not return a fair portion to God? The position of Elder is the highest in the congregation and is not to be taken lightly.

When we assemble with the other saints on the first day of the week, we remember the sacrifice Christ made for us, we give thanks to God for all His blessings, and we praise and glorify His name and participate in the workings and the growth of the church; we are doing well those things it takes to be pleasing to the Lord.

Paul had thoughts on this subject.

"Be ye therefore followers of God, as dear children: And walk in love, as Christ also hath loved us, and hath given Himself for us an offering and a sacrifice to God for a sweetsmelling savour" (Ephesians 5:1-2).

Following God and walking in love one to another will add to our strength of faith.

"Till we all come in the unity of the faith, and of the knowledge of the Son of God, unto a perfect man, unto the measure of the stature of the fullness of Christ: That we henceforth be no more children, tossed to and fro, and carried about with every wind of doctrine, by the slight of men,

72

and cunning craftiness, whereby they lie in wait to deceive" (Ephesians 4:14-15).

"Finally, my brethren, be strong in the Lord, and in the power of His might. Put on the whole armor of God, that ye may be able to stand against the wiles of the devil" (Ephesians 6:10-11).

We could reference many more scriptures about the Christian life, but these are sufficient to make our point. We refer often to Paul, one of the great teachers and writers in Bible times, and he pretty much summed it up when he wrote to the Ephesians.

"Therefore I, a prisoner for serving the Lord, beg you to lead a life worthy of your calling, for you have been called by God. Always be humble and gentle, be patient with each other, making allowance for each other's faults because of your love. Make every effort to keep yourselves united in the spirit binding yourselves together with peace" (Ephesians 4:1-3, NLT).

CHAPTER 14

A couple more thoughts worthy of our consideration, and we will bring this writing to a close. It is unfortunate that too many people today do not have the concern about Bible teaching that should be important to them. There are some who absolutely deny the fact of God, heaven and hell, and eternity. It is our hope that those who read this book will be convinced that these things are fact. There is a God, *the* God, creator of all that exists in the world. There is a final phase of living called eternity. There is a place called heaven and a place called hell. They are just as real as the sun, moon, and the stars we see in the sky. The Lord teaches us that when our life on this earth is finished, we will move on into the eternity which will consist of two parts or realms, one in the presence of our God and the saved, the other reserved for the lost who will endure eternal suffering. Paul reminded Timothy that Jesus would be the one who would be the judge (2 Timothy 4:1). "For the Father judgeth no man, but hath committed all judgment to the Son" (John 5:22). Whether one chooses to believe this or not does not change truth; they are real and denying them does not alter the truth that each of us will be relegated to one or the other. Very simply put, one will have to make a choice of destinations based on what they choose to believe or do nothing and let the choice be made for them. As we noted earlier, there can be no doubt about the time when judgment will be made, and the results will be forthcoming. To the Romans, Paul wrote:

"But because you are stubborn and refused to turn from your sin, you are storing up terrible punishment for yourself. For a day of anger is coming when God's righteous judgment will be revealed. He will judge everyone according to what they have done. He will give eternal life to those who keep on doing good, seeking after the glory and honor and immortality that God offers. But he will pour out his anger and wrath on those who live for themselves, who refuse to obey the truth and instead live lives of wickedness. There will be trouble and calamity for everyone who keeps on doing what is evil, for the Jew first and also for the gentile. But there will be glory and honor and peace from God for all who do good, for the Jew first and also for the gentile, for God does not show favoritism" (Romans 2:5-11, NLT).

This is not the way He wants it to be. Paul said they had hard hearts and were stubborn and instead of repenting and turning to God, they continued in sin. Jew or gentile, it makes no difference, failing to repent will lead to destruction. To the Thessalonians:

"To you who are troubled rest with us, when the Lord Jesus shall be revealed from heaven with

His mighty angels, in flaming fire, taking venge-
ance on them that know not God, and that obey
not the gospel of our Lord Jesus Christ" (2
Thessalonians 1:7-8).

These are sobering thoughts and not to be ignored, they are speaking to all, saint and sinner alike. The writer of the Hebrew letter was writing to people who are Christians; listen to his warning:

"Dear friends, if we deliberately continue sin-
ning after we have received knowledge of the
truth, there is no longer any sacrifice that will
cover these sins. There is only the terrible ex-
pectation of God's judgment and the raging fire
that will consume his enemies" (Hebrews
10:26-27, NLT).

"For it is impossible to bring back to repent-
ance those who were once enlightened, those
who have experienced the good things of
heaven and shared in the Holy Spirit, who have
tasted the goodness of the word of God and the
power of the age to come, and who then turn
away from God. It is impossible to bring such
people back to repentance; by rejecting the Son
of God, they themselves are nailing Him to the
cross once again and holding Him up to public
shame" (Hebrews 6:4-6, NLT).

These truths should strike terror into the minds of thinking people. They speak of the loss of soul for which there is no reprieve. Peter's words were compelling also:

> *"For if after they have escaped the pollutions of the world through the knowledge of the Lord and savior Jesus Christ, they are again entangled therein, and overcome, the latter end is worse with them than the beginning. For it had been better for them not to have known the way of righteousness, than, after they have known it, to turn from the holy commandment delivered unto them" (2 Peter 2:20-21).*

There can be no question of the validity of these statements which came by the direction of the Holy Spirit. The truth is set forth to warn Christians and others as well. We cannot deny God and expect that He will be happy about it. We cannot deny that Jesus has given us truth and time to prepare for the coming judgment. Is there a possibility that these scriptures disagree with others? Absolutely not. There is never any disagreement in the Bible instruction. We know that everyone sins: "For all have sinned and come short of the glory of God" (Romans 3:23). Paul said that every one of us are sinners, and if that is true (and it is true, Paul the man of God had this truth from the Holy Spirit), then we are doomed. It's possible but not absolute. To reconcile these thoughts, we must bring in more of the Bible text.

John wrote:

"We are writing these things so that you may fully share our joy. This is the message we heard from Jesus and now declare to you: God is light and there is no darkness in him at all. So we are lying if we say we have fellowship with God but go on living in spiritual darkness we are not practicing the truth" (1 John 1:4-6, NLT).

"If we say that we have no sin, we deceive our-selves, and the truth is not in us. If we confess our sins, He is faithful and just to forgive us our sins, and to cleanse us from all unrighteous-ness" (1 John 1:8-10).

"My little children, these things write I unto you, that ye sin not. And if any man sin, we have an advocate with the father, Jesus Christ the righteous"(1 John 2:1).

So, now we know the answer. It is entirely possible for someone to become so engrossed in sin that they do not want to repent and turn to God, or their heart is so hardened that they will not return to God. In that case there is no question, that person will have lost their soul when it comes to the time of judgment. But John has shown us that we can sin, and that it's most likely we will. Paul says that all of us do sin, but we have a way to overcome this if we choose it. If we will repent and ask God to forgive us, He will allow us to return to the fold to be once again cleansed from sin; we know Jesus will cleanse us again. Nonetheless, we need to be ex-tremely cautious and be living as much as is humanly possible free from sin and remembering that we do have Jesus and his blood, which will cleanse us again if we repent and pray. So, there is no misunderstanding, we now know that it is not imperative that anyone should be lost. There is no logical reason for any person to look to the time of judgment with mortal fear. Will there be those who will be eternally lost forever? The Bible says there will be because some will resist God's saving grace. That is not what God wants, but it will happen. Jesus said:

> *"He that rejecteth me, and receiveth not my words, hath one that judgeth him: the word that I have spoken, the same shall judge him in the last day" (John 12:48).*

Jesus will be the one who will judge. When Paul told the Romans and Philippians that sooner or later every knee would bow and every tongue would confess that Jesus is the Son of God, he was not using words to fill space; they were factual notification of what lay ahead for all of mankind.

> *"For we must all appear before the judgment seat of Christ; that every one may receive the things done in his body, according to that he hath done, whether it be good or bad" (2 Corinthians 5:10).*

Again, the words of the Hebrew letter:

"If the word spoken by angels was steadfast, and every transgression and disobedience received a just recompence of reward; how shall we escape, if we neglect so great salvation?" (Hebrews 2:2).

The answer is simple; neglect the invitation and pay the price. There will be no escape for the impenitent. We have used enough scripture to remove any doubt about the time of judgment; it will happen. Paul told the Athenians:

"He hath appointed a day, in the which He will judge the world in righteousness by that man whom He hath ordained; whereof He hath given assurance unto all men, in that He hath raised him from the dead" (Acts 17:31).

One more thought from Peter, and we will move on.

"For the time is come that judgment must begin at the House of God: and if it first begin at us, what shall the end be of them that obey not the gospel of God? And if the righteous scarcely be saved, where shall the ungodly and the sinner appear? (1 Peter 4:17-18).

CHAPTER 15

We have in no wise exhausted all the teaching in God's word about love and about life. From what we have studied so far, we have a much better understanding of the depth and purpose of love and what that means to us and how it contributes to a joyful, peaceful, serene life if we allow Jesus to be our guide. David was fully aware of the value of this leadership from above. He knew he would be lead in the paths of righteousness, that he need not have fear of evil, that he could walk through the valley of the shadow of death and everything would be alright; and because of this faith he knew that goodness and mercy would be with him in this lifetime and that he would dwell in the house of the Lord forever (Psalm 23). What a comforting realization this is to all who choose to believe God's word and desire eternal life in His heaven.

In 1745, William Williams a Connecticut politician and businessman published a beautiful hymn that for many decades has been a favorite of this writer.

> *"Guide me oh thou Great Jehovah,*
> *pilgrim through this barren land.*
> *I am weak but thou art mighty,*
> *hold me with thy powerful hand."*

Among other things Williams was a minister and a signatory on the Declaration of Independence. What strength we derive from knowing that the power of the

Almighty God is guiding our way through this life and beyond if we will allow Him to do so.

Because of His love and mercy God wishes that all will be in heaven with Him. However, because of unbelief, sin, and stubbornness, many will refuse to permit the great God to be the leader of their lives. This God, the one true and living God, desires that all would come to repentance and be saved, but not all will do so. God has the power to send sinners that do not obey His will to eternal condemnation. Luke was aware of this power in the very early times of Christ. He quotes Jesus:

"And I say unto you my friends, be not afraid of them that kill the body, and after that have no more that they can do. But I will forewarn you whom ye shall fear: Fear him, which after he hath killed hath power to cast into hell; yea I say unto you, fear him" (Luke 12:4-5).

We have stated this repeatedly and will continue to do so: There is a heaven, and Jesus has gone to prepare it for the saved. There is a hell, and it is just as real as the heaven we believe in, and unfortunately, there will be those who will be relegated to that realm of suffering eternally because they refused to accept the love of God. What a terrible thing that will be, and tragic because it is avoidable. Nobody would wish to suffer eternally, but it will happen. God cannot be anything other than true to every man, so He cannot be a respecter of persons, all will be treated equally, so deny God, be disobedient, pay the price.

"For God did not even spare the angels who sinned. He threw them into hell, in gloomy pits of darkness where they are being held until the day of judgment" (2 Peter 2:4, NLT).

"So you see, the Lord knows how to rescue godly people from their trials, even while keeping the wicked under punishment until the day of final judgment" (2 Peter 2:9, NLT).

Jesus said there is a hell, do we question His word? Only the foolish would. There is a place called hell. When teaching from the mountain, Jesus stated: "but whosoever shall say, Thou fool, shall be in danger of hell fire" (Matthew 5:22b). Again, the words of Jesus:

"Just as the weeds are sorted out and burned in the fire, so it will be at the end of the world. The son of man will send his angels, and they will remove from His Kingdom everything that causes sin and all who do evil. And the angels will throw them into the fiery furnace where there will be weeping and gnashing of teeth" (Matthew 13:40-42).

"That is the way it will be at the end of the world. The angels will come and separate the wicked people from the righteous, throwing the wicked into the fiery furnace, where there will be weeping and gnashing of teeth. Do you understand these things?" (Matthew 13:49-51).

That is the consequential question. Do we understand what was said? Do we believe it is true, and have we reacted in a positive manner? This is where the consequences appear: believe and obey and be rewarded. Do not believe or choose to ignore truth and pay the price: eternal suffering. Jesus described hell as a place of eternal torment, eternal suffering and unhappiness, and it is the realm in which the wicked will be banished.

> *"Marvel not at this: for the hour is coming, in the which all that are in the graves shall hear His voice, and shall come forth; they that have done good, unto the resurrection of life; and they that have done evil, to the resurrection of damnation" (John 5:28-29).*

What more can be said? Certainly, there are many more passages of scripture which we could consider on our subjects: passages of encouragement, passages of warning, but for the most part it would be repetitious of what has already been studied. We can only say so many times that we are here on this earth for one primary reason, and that is to prepare for eternity. It is possible to achieve many things while we live, accomplishments such as happiness, families, careers, temporal situations which are a part of our life, and are to a great degree very worthwhile. We support families, do good to others, make our loved ones feel safe and free, but as we have repeatedly stated, there is only one accomplishment in the end that will be of lasting value. This one truly significant merit is to be making our life right with God. We accomplish this by believing in the fact that there is a God, the creator of all that exists. We have faith in the truth that Jesus Christ, the Son of God, was willing to give His life as a sacrifice for sin. Know that our lives will only be complete and that we can be freed from the penalty of sin by accepting Christ as our Savior. Let it be known that we have faith in His promise of salvation. When we arrive at this point then we know we must be baptized for the remission of the sins in our life; we are then added to His church, His Kingdom on earth and then the preparation to meet Him begins in earnest. Live righteous lives, do good unto others, love mankind, grow and gain strength by a dedicated prayer life, and God will be with us in our every effort for good. God bless you for reading this book, and it is the prayer of the author that your life will be one of contentment, happy, productive, and finally, pleasing to God.

EPILOGUE

I would ask your indulgence for another minute or two to say a bit about this book. This is the tenth book in a series of lessons from God's word which have been written by the grace of God and with a lot of help from Him and my beloved wife, Juanita. Our hope is that with each of the books maybe someone would be led to Christ and maybe another might be strengthened and re-dedicate their lives to serving the Living God. We feel that we have been blessed with the opportunity of giving many hundreds of copies to those who wish to read them and blessed because we have done so. They have been used for classroom teaching, one-on-one instruction and when ordered in quantities, we sell them at cost plus shipping.

Two of the books are made up of articles the author has written for a Christian publication entitled *The Quarterly*. Anyone reading this would greatly benefit themselves by subscribing to that publication. It is issued four times per year and is inexpensive. Each issue is literally filled to the brim with timely articles to help the reader to grow in the faith, to be of help to others and prepare their own future needs. Subscribe or find individual issues at www.CobbPublishing.com.

We have little or nothing to do with how long we will be here on earth. God is in control, and that is all with which we should be concerned. The author is in his ninety-fourth year, and it is entirely possible this will be the final book written. However, we cannot be knowledgeable about what God's plans might be, so if time permits and a subject comes up, perhaps there could be another. Whatever the case might be, I am thankful to God for the privilege He has provided me to be able to write. I am thankful that my wife Juanita has been always with me to encourage and help. I am thankful for my brother and friend Bradley Cobb for publishing my work and allowing me to be one of the writers for *The Quarterly*. To all who encounter this work, I wish for God's blessings to be bountiful for each of you and hope that each will sincerely dedicate themselves to preparing for the future.

Made in the USA
Monee, IL
22 October 2023

44998887R00056